Therefore, Hope

A Mom's Journey in Loss and Hope

Janet Lindsey

WESTBOW®
PRESS
A DIVISION OF THOMAS NELSON
& ZONDERVAN

Cover Photo: Laura Faust

Unless otherwise noted, Scripture is taken from the Holy Bible, New International Version.

Copyright ©1973, 1978, 1984 by International Bible Society. Used by permission of Zondervan Publishing House. All rights reserved.

Scripture quotations marked NLT are taken from the Holy Bible, New Living Translation, copyright © 1996, 2004, 2007 by Tyndale House Foundation. Used by permission of Tyndale House Publishers, Inc., Carol Stream, Illinois 60188. All rights reserved.

Scripture quotations marked NASB are taken from the New American Standard Bible®. Copyright © 1960, 1962, 1963, 1968, 1971, 1972, 1973, 1975, 1977, 1995 by The Lockman Foundation. Used by permission of *www.Lockman.org*.

Scripture quotations marked KJV are taken from the King James Version of the Bible. The World Publishing Company. Public Domain

WestBow Press books may be ordered through booksellers or by contacting:

WestBow Press
A Division of Thomas Nelson & Zondervan
1663 Liberty Drive
Bloomington, IN 47403
www.westbowpress.com
1 (866) 928-1240

ISBN: 978-1-4908-5895-1 (sc)
ISBN: 978-1-4908-5894-4 (e)

Library of Congress Control Number: 2014956170

Printed in the United States of America.
WestBow Press rev. date: 11/03/2014

Dedication

For my parents, who gave us a godly heritage. Your
prayers and encouragement have strengthened
us in our journey. You have laughed and cried
with us. Your love is a constant support.

Yet this I call to mind and therefore I have hope:
Because of the LORD'S great love we are
not consumed, for his compassions never fail.
They are new every morning; great is your faithfulness.
—Lamentations 3:21–23

Contents

Introduction

Yet this I call to mind and therefore I have
hope (Lam. 3:21).

Hope is a matter of living or dying. Without it, there is
despair and darkness. With it, we can live even in the midst
of sorrow and find the peace that Jesus offers. Hope is not
wishful thinking, but unseen reality. It is a sure confidence—
an assurance a Christian has for things not yet revealed, but
that ultimately will be seen. Of course, the opposite of hope
is hopelessness. What a broad gulf lies in between.

Who lives without hope? Do we not all hope for
something? If we are in what seems like a hopeless estate,
we are in despair and pitifully sad. Our hearts appear
broken beyond repair. Still, we don't have to travel through
life without hope. There is only one true source of hope
and that is Jesus. All other ways will continually fail and
disappoint you.

In 2009, my husband, Ed, and I lost our twenty-
two-year-old son and only child, Gary. He was an avid
sportsman, but he especially loved fishing. One afternoon,
he went out in his boat alone to scout for an upcoming

fishing tournament. It was a cool, very windy April day. The lake was extremely rough. Somehow (and we do not know how), he fell out of the boat. Although he was an excellent swimmer and in great physical condition, the cold water, layers of clothes, and the apparently swift current were too much for him. For three days and nights, they searched for our precious son, finding him the day before Easter Sunday.

Our world seemed to come to an end. How could we possibly go on without him? We were devastated beyond words. At times, we felt hopeless, as if we couldn't continue living. Except for the Lord's strength and gracious mercy, we might have collapsed from the grief. He gave us hope to endure, while comforting us in His embrace.

On September 11, 2001, most of us remember where we were when the news of the attacks came. Like most Americans, I was glued to the television. We watched in horror as terrorists took thousands of lives from men, women, and children. Since that day, Americans have been keenly aware of the threat of possible terrorist attacks anytime and anywhere. We have tightened security in many areas. The devastation from weather, earthquakes, and crime has become frequent and widespread. Indifference, divorce, and the destruction of the family are common. As I write this, we have several close friends who are battling serious, life-threatening illnesses. Life shakes us to the core, along with the realization that life is uncertain, life is painful, and life can seem hopeless.

In the book of Lamentations, Jeremiah wrote more than three chapters on the devastation and horrors that took place after the destruction of Jerusalem. The events he described caused him great sorrow; some are beyond my comprehension. However, in the midst of such tragedy, Jeremiah recalled that God is good, and with Him, there is hope.

God is good because of His love and compassion. Even in our darkest days, God is faithful "to those whose hope is in him" (Lam. 3:25).

Several months before our son's accident, I had tests run for stomach issues. Not having felt well for a while, the doctor also scheduled preventative tests that are common for people of fifty. The appointment for the tests happened to fall the week after my son's death, so I cancelled it. I was physically, emotionally, and mentally unable to go through any tests. At that point, my health didn't seem like a concern. I was immersed in an attitude of *I don't care about myself.* I felt helpless; life seemed hopeless. Why carry on? I didn't have the enthusiasm or will to do so. What was the point? My heart lost its strength, my body physically ached, and my soul was in anguish.

Then one day I read Lamentations 3:22. The words, "we are not consumed" jumped off the page and landed in my heart. The reason we are not consumed, the writer explained, is "because of the LORD'S great love …for his compassions never fail." My God has compassion and love for me. He gave His one and only Son, so He is able to comfort me in the loss of my only son. God spoke to me through this verse and let me know I wasn't going to die of my grief. He was going to make sure I wasn't consumed to the point of giving up. He showed me the hope I needed to carry on, and this hope was found in Him.

We have an anchor when life is good and going well and when it falls apart right before our eyes. It is our anchor of hope secured in God (Heb. 6:19). So secure that "though the earth give way and the mountains fall into the heart of the sea" (Ps. 46:2), we will not fear. It is an unshaken hope (Heb. 12:28). No matter what happens on this earth or to us, there is a confidence in knowing that God is our help, our strength, and our place to hide (Ps. 46:1 and Ps. 32:7). He has promised His believers a resting hope of eternal life, and He does not and cannot lie (Titus 1:2). God is love, and love "always hopes" (1 Cor. 13:7).

Worldly hope will disappoint you every time. It may last for a season, but placing hope in your job, the government, your material possessions, or another person will eventually fail you. It is temporary, and when it fails, it brings despair. For my husband and me, our hopes and dreams for our future on earth with our son are gone. They've been shattered. In order to keep from despairing, I remind myself of the Lord's faithfulness, His great love and His compassions that are fresh every morning (Lam. 3:22–23). God never runs out on you. When all else fails, He will not. He has not forsaken me, and He will not forsake you. If you are experiencing a time when you feel you have no hope, remember God, the author of hope. His hope endures forever. His hope is lasting and faithful. With every trial and test that comes into our lives, if we trust that our heavenly Father has knowledge, purpose, and control over them and allow Him to work through them, then we will find our love for God has increased. Our knowledge of Him after those trials will be greater.

My qualification for offering hope comes from my own experience of loss and the anguish of my heart. The need to find hope in my darkest time, when all seemed hopeless, was overpowering. My search for hope drew me closer to the only One who can offer lasting hope. His Word is life and strength, and He gave me the will to go on. Having hope was a matter of living or dying.

When I think of all of God's attributes derived from hope, I am not overwhelmed by the sorrows of this life. Instead, I am overwhelmed by God. "Faith is the confidence that what we hope for will actually happen; it gives us assurance about things we cannot see" (Heb. 11:1 NLT). "Yet this I call to mind …" (Lam. 3:21) is saying to remember, to reflect as often as necessary on all the ways God has given us hope. We as believers have so much to look forward to. We will have a perfect, beautiful eternal home. We will see Jesus face to face and praise Him continually. We will see our believing loved ones and never again be separated from them. We will be happy and never again cry tears of sadness. We will never be sick or exhausted. We will be at rest and peace forevermore. Therefore, hope.

Chapter 1

Unfamiliar Territory

I will lead the blind by ways they have not known, along unfamiliar paths I will guide them; I will turn the darkness into light before them and make the rough places smooth. These are the things I will do; I will not forsake them (Isa. 42:16).

Grief. The anguish and affliction from our deep sorrow became a daily companion. It hovered over us, engulfed us, and sometimes shut us down for a period of time. Although we did not understand it at the beginning, we were embarking on a journey of grief that would change the rest of our lives.

This grief has been unrelenting at times, without respect to our schedules or plans. It has come in and taken precedence over every emotion and thought. It crushed our dreams for our son and his future. At times it has captured every fiber of our being. It has taken us down a path we have never traveled before. We don't always understand what we are feeling or even if it is an emotion distinctive to grief. At times we struggle with thinking we might be losing our minds or just losing *it* altogether. Grief has tested our resolve, our endurance, our character, and most importantly, our faith in God. It is the essence of sadness.

So what do I do with my grief? How do I grasp this insistent power that wants to overtake me? I will use it for the glory of God. *But wait*, you say. *Wasn't it God who allowed this tragedy in the first place? Could He not have prevented this and spared us all this anguish?* The answers to those questions are yes and yes. Somewhere in this path of grief, I had to settle in my heart and mind that God is sovereign. I may not understand; I may ask why, but there is comfort in knowing that God, who is in control of the universe, is the God who created us and loves us with an everlasting love. He knows more about us than we know ourselves. Whether or not we understand His purposes, He is still sovereign. "Though he brings grief, he will show compassion, so great is his unfailing love" (Lam. 3:32).

Do we believe He can help us in our sorrows and suffering? He will show compassion, for it is one of His attributes. Job is the greatest example we have of grief and suffering in the Bible. He didn't see the bigger picture and neither do we. And that is an important reality to bear in mind: there is a bigger picture. God has eternal purposes. We tend to think of the here and now, although everything we do here and now has eternal purposes.

There have been many instances when this unfamiliar territory of intense grief has nearly raged out of control.

On my way to the cemetery one day, I took the same path we traveled the day of Gary's funeral. In my mind, I was following the hearse again. The thought of my child lying in a coffin and riding in the back of that vehicle on the way to his burial overcame me. Never would he have imagined even a week earlier that this is where he would be. Most twenty-two-year-olds don't think that way. It is an exciting time when they have their whole life ahead of them. My chest was aching as I felt sorry for my son. I wanted to make everything right. I wanted to change it all. It was a horrible, helpless feeling. I wept the rest of the way until I reached his grave.

The Lord gave me great comfort while standing in the cemetery that day. He reminded me that Gary wasn't riding in that hearse, and he wasn't lying in the ground. Only the shell of his earthly body was there. While we were going through the motions of a burial on earth, he was experiencing the joy of heaven. My child was completely happy and safe in the presence of Jesus. Now, this reality gives me great comfort. However, it doesn't take away my feelings of loss. I miss my son more than words can express. I yearn for him every day. My grief, though, can be used to help so many others on their unfamiliar paths of sorrow. It can be used to bring good out of immense loss. Ed and I have a persistent need to have good come from our loss. Gary's death was not in vain. God will use it for good and for His purposes.

Chapter 2

I'm a Mess

Consider him who endured such opposition
from sinful men, so that you will not grow
weary and lose heart (Heb. 12:3).

One morning, I was looking through pictures of my
son from a fishing tournament. He was holding a
check from winnings received for first place and *lunker*
(largest) fish. My eyes fell on his hands. An overwhelming
yearning came over me to hold his hands. I needed to feel
them, examine every inch, and hold them close to my face.
I became frustrated just knowing I couldn't even pick up the
phone and hear his voice.

When death takes a loved one, the separation seems
unbearable at times. The frustration comes from knowing
there is absolutely nothing to be done about it. I can't have
that happiness of being near my son. *Lord, I just want to
hear his voice! Touch his hands!* I'm tired and worn out from

all the different emotions running through me. Trying to analyze all of them is wearing me down.

I began to have organizational issues. I have always been a neat housekeeper, with things in their place within a clean home. After my son's death, I became quite disorganized. My office had papers scattered everywhere that needed to be filed away. I would see something requiring my attention, but all I could do was make a pile. I had piles all over the house. My concentration waned, and my ability to stay with a task for more than a few minutes was gone. I would start one chore, and before I finished, start another one—failing to complete either of them. Getting sidetracked was a constant problem. I kept forgetting what I needed to do and ended up doing something else. Later, I would find my disorganized mess and wonder how I could have forgotten about it.

There was also the matter of motivation. I would get inspired about a project and start into it full force. In a few days, I was completely uninterested in the venture and couldn't muster any enthusiasm whatsoever to carry it out. A similar thing frequently happened when I went shopping. It didn't matter whether it was for clothes or household items, I would really like something, purchase it, and within a week or two, the desire was gone and I was ready to take it back.

Shortly after our son's death, I wanted to go to a local greenhouse to purchase some plants. Being an independent person, I was amazed at how paralyzed I felt this day. I pulled into the parking lot and just sat there. The thought of going into a crowd of people overwhelmed me, even while I hated the feeling of being alone. I started crying and drove home. I needed help functioning that day. Ed took me back to the greenhouse and stayed by my side. I needed his presence and support. This may sound trivial to someone who hasn't experienced grief, but I vividly remember it as a day of confusion and helplessness.

My whole outlook on life was numbed. Some days, I felt I just existed. The constant wear on my body, soul, and mind was pressing down and paralyzing me. I wanted the strength and will to live, but I couldn't find them. I needed the Lord's help to pull me out of the directionless, unmotivated state I was in. Isaiah said God "gives strength to the weary" (Isa. 40:29), and we "will walk and not be faint" (Isa. 40:31). I knew I needed this kind of help.

"Consider him" (Heb. 12:3). I think of Jesus, whose life was a sorrowful one. "He was despised and rejected by men, a man of sorrows, and familiar with suffering" (Isa. 53:3). He came to earth knowing He was going to die for those who loved Him *and* those who hated Him. He kept to the task, all the while knowing the end result. He went about His Father's business—healing the sick, feeding the hungry, bringing sight to the blind, and sound to the deaf—while teaching that the kingdom of God had come. He fulfilled His purpose on earth, and He is the one who could help me with all my messes and disorganized life so as not to lose heart.

I began asking God to help me concentrate on one task at a time and to organize my day according to His plans. I sought His help to keep my mind focused on Him and my eternal home, with an understanding that the frustrations caused by the separation from my son were temporary. I still have piles of messes at times, but I have tucked some of them away for a later day. The Lord helped me understand that the piles weren't nearly as important as living each day for Him.

Chapter 3

Jesus Questions Me

I was astonished one morning while reading my devotions. There was question after question that Jesus asked specific people. It was astonishing because the questions came from several different devotionals. I gradually realized Jesus was talking to me through each question He asked. It became a very personal worship time in which I found myself trying to answer each question from my heart.

"Woman, why are you crying?" (John 20:15). In Mary Magdalene's sorrow over losing her beloved Christ, she was overcome with grief. She had come to the tomb before daylight, probably after not having slept all night, to anoint Jesus' body. Mary's love for her Lord was strong and real. She had been forgiven much. She loved much, but then, I imagine she might have felt deserted and alone. When Jesus asked her this question, He was mindful of her tears, was aware of her grief, and wanted to assure her of His resurrection.

This passage became personal to me. God is the "Father of compassion and the God of all comfort" (2 Cor. 1:3).

He is attentive to my sorrow—every shed tear—and one day, He will personally wipe away every tear from my eyes (Rev. 21:4). I have cried thousands of tears in the last five years. I miss my son. His absence is constantly with me. The thought of *might have been but will never be* whirls in my mind. I have also cried tears for others who are experiencing loss. God has given me a compassion for other sufferers. I want them to realize that because Jesus was resurrected, assuring us we will be, too, we shouldn't "grieve like people who have no hope" (1 Thess. 4:13 NLT).

There is a biblical story of a woman who just lost her only son (Luke 7:11–17 NLT). Her sorrow was deep for her only child, and it was even greater because she was a widow. The funeral procession included a large crowd of friends offering comfort. Jesus saw her, and "his heart overflowed with compassion. 'Don't cry!' he said. Then he walked over to the coffin and touched it." Oh, the tenderness of our Lord and His empathy in our suffering. He chose to raise this son back to life for his mother. He chose for me to trust Him that my son is alive and well in heaven. And this is the future of all those who place their trust in Jesus. The grave is a resting place for our bodies; it is not our home. Jesus wants us to be confident in this.

"Why are you so afraid?" (Matt. 8:26). The disciples and Jesus were in a boat when a terrible storm came on the lake. But Jesus was sleeping while the waves came over the boat, rocking everyone about. They woke Him up so that He could save them. They doubted themselves, but they had been with Jesus enough to know that He could handle this storm.

Isn't that what we do when we first see signs of trouble? Cry out to Jesus to do something? I have been with Jesus a long time, but when the shadow of death was around me, I found myself afraid—afraid of this strange helplessness and the thoughts that tortured me. I was afraid of this new depth of emotion and the feelings of loss that I couldn't put into words. And I was afraid for my son.

When Jesus was on the way to Jairus' house to heal his daughter, the report came that she had already died. Jesus immediately responded to the man's first emotion concerning his daughter and said, "Don't be afraid" (Mark 5:36). Death is frightening, especially when it happens to your child, the one whom you've taken care of, protected, and wanted the best for. You wonder, *is he okay?* Even if the child is in heaven, you wonder. It is also terrifying because of what your child had to go through before death.

I was afraid of the unknown journey I was embarking upon. However, the one who can calm any storm was asking the questions about fear. *Why are you so afraid? What is the cause of your fear? Are you afraid of the effects of your fears? Are you afraid of darkness, of evil? Do you have faith in Me to meet your fears?*

I am not a theologian, but I see a beautiful picture in this passage from Matthew 8:23–27. First, the disciples followed Jesus into the boat. They were His followers. They believed in who He was and were willing to devote their lives to Him. They had established a relationship with Him.

Second, Jesus remained calm during the storm, while the others panicked in fear. Jesus can sustain us and uphold us during the storms of life. He's not asleep in the back of the boat. He may not take away our storms, but He can grant calm in the chaos. Even in my grief, He has granted a peace of heart that can't be explained.

Third, the disciples cried out for Jesus to save them. They had just witnessed the healing of many before they got into the boat; they knew to call on the one who performed miracles. It is good for me to remember the faithfulness of the Lord in the past, so as to increase my faith for the present. When I am overtaken with sorrow, I cry out, *Where are You, God?* But I can be assured of His presence with me.

Fourth, Jesus spoke to the storm, and it was *completely* calm. The Creator of the universe has control over it, and all He has to do is speak, and creation obeys. He can be trusted.

Lastly, the disciples were amazed. Some of them were fishermen and had seen storms before, but they had never witnessed one stop instantly on command.

Know this: Jesus has control over our storms. He is in the boat with us. "So do not fear, for I am with you; do not be dismayed, for I am your God. I will strengthen you and help you; I will uphold you with my righteous right hand" (Isa. 41:10).

Ed has made the comment so many times about the songs we sing in church referencing storms and how they involve the sea or water. One song in particular talks about not going under. Our minds tend to wonder where we do not want them to go, and that is, our son in the water for three days and nights, not knowing where he was or what happened to him. It is too much to bear. Even writing this is hard. I doubt anyone else thinks like we do when we sing these songs. They have a different meaning for us. My comfort is in knowing that Jesus was in the boat with Gary, and when he went under, Jesus never left him alone. He calmed his fears, upheld him, and took him straight to his heavenly home.

"Why did you doubt?" (Matt. 14:31). Right after our son's accident, I doubted God's love and watch-care over us. I had prayed that day for my son's safety, as I had every day. I was angry with God for not protecting him and sparing his life. I began to think I couldn't trust Him. He didn't answer my prayers the way *I* wanted. Instead, He took my most precious possession.

Before Jesus asked why there was doubt, He stated the reason for the doubt—little faith.

But Lord, I thought my faith was strong? It was strong for my life the way it was, but now I needed more faith. I had been through the trial of faith; now I needed the courage of faith. My faith was true but needed to be proven. My faith in God needed to grow.

In this passage from Matthew, Peter walks on water until he takes his eyes off Jesus and focuses on the storm. He had faith, or else he never would have gotten out of the boat. But, it needed to grow.

Storms have a way of increasing our faith. They show us the great depths of our neediness. They reveal our helplessness. Storms awaken us to take a good look at our faith. Where is it? How great is it? Jesus said, "If you have faith as small as a mustard seed, you can say to this mountain, 'Move from here to there' and it will move. Nothing will be impossible for you" (Matt.17:20).

I no longer doubt God's love or care for me. Lack of understanding of my circumstances doesn't make me doubt His faithfulness. He has never left me. He has made me aware of His presence many times and has given me tangible evidence of His attentiveness to my situation. But even if He had not, His Word is proof enough. What He says, He does, and He wants us to have faith in Him. Step out into the water; it won't part until you do.

"And why do you worry?" (Matt. 6: 28a). It does us no good. This is one truth that came home to me after our son's passing. All those years I worried about him were for nothing. When he was small, I worried about him being so active and hurting himself. When he started school, I worried about his school work and making friends. As he grew older, I worried about the negative influences on his life. When he started driving, I had big worries. And the list goes on. I can sound spiritual and say I was really just concerned, but the truth is, I worried. I prayed and I worried. It is so hard not to worry.

But Jesus tells us we shouldn't worry. If He cares enough about our basic needs, such as food and clothes, will He not care for our children? He even said that He cared so much for the birds and the flowers that He met their needs, adding, "Are you not much more valuable than they?" (Matt. 6:26b). Why do we not trust him to take care of us? Is it because we are afraid something will happen to our children or to us, and we want to be able to keep control? Here is another truth that came to me immediately after our son went missing. I had no control over the situation. I desperately needed to do something to find him. The realization that I was not in control was overpowering. I was totally dependent on God. It was out of my hands and in His. Even if life doesn't turn out like we planned or purposed, in whose hands do we want to be?

While standing over my son's casket, this control thing consumed me. I felt a total helplessness that there was absolutely nothing I could have done to prevent his death.

I had no way of knowing beforehand. I was at the mercy of God Almighty, the one who knew from before time began how that tragic day would turn out. It was a helplessness that led me straight to the one who was in control, the one who could meet every need. It's a paradox. The God who created us with needs wants us to come to Him so He can meet those needs. Jesus said, "I am the gate; whoever enters through me will be saved. He will come in and go out, and find pasture" (John 10:9), meaning, all our needs will be met.

I worried all those years for nothing. I think this is what Jesus is trying to tell us in Matthew 6:33 when He says, "But seek first his kingdom and his righteousness, and all these things will be given to you as well." By centering our lives on Him, He will take care of all our physical, mental, emotional, and spiritual needs. He is able.

"What do you want me to do for you?" (Luke 18:41). The blind beggar begs for mercy. He wanted to see, and he knew Jesus could heal him. He believed in who Jesus was and kept calling over and over again, "Jesus, Son of David" (v. 38NLT), implying he knew Jesus as Messiah. The crowd tried to quiet him, "but he shouted all the more" (v. 39). He was desperate for Jesus. And Jesus responded. This question, "What do you want me to do for you?" is personal and engaging. Even though God knows our deepest needs, He still wants us to ask Him to meet those needs.

"What do you want me to do for *you*?"

My prayer is,

Lord, I want to know You in a deeper way. Sometimes I feel so much despair and lose my will to go on. Help me not to lose hope but to live above my circumstances, knowing that You have my life under Your control. You are gracious and merciful. Uphold me with Your righteousness. Calm my fears; grant me strength and courage. I am desperate for You. You are Messiah!

Chapter 4

Keeper of My Soul

Deep calls to deep (Ps. 42:7a).

There have been times when I wallowed in my sorrow. I kept Jesus at arm's length and wanted Him to stay back and let me feel sorry for myself. All the while, He yearned for me to come to Him. He is the *deep* calling to the pain in my heart. He wants to meet my needs and reveal Himself, giving me a deeper understanding of His love, if only I will come.

The greatest example I can think of to describe this is my relationship to my son. Oh, how I love my son! I always wanted to meet his needs while he was here and provide him with love. I did what I could to make his life the best it could be. Sometimes he would even ask for advice, which I was always ready to give. Since he is not physically here now, I have a continual yearning to talk to him. I want to know what he is doing, whom he has met and talked with, where he is living, and so many more heavenly things. I want to touch him, smell him, hug him, and just sit for a while and enjoy his presence. I would even take ten seconds if God would grant it.

My heavenly Father yearns to be with me. His love for me is greater than my love for my son, although that is beyond my comprehension. How I long for my son, but how much more my God longs for me. He desires to spend time with me. He wants to guide me from beginning to end. His *deep* is full of everything I need, every day, if only I will take the unhurried time to be with Him. I would probably never have realized this longing of God's to the extent that I do had I not experienced great loss.

Another great comfort I have is that His Spirit prays for me. When I am in deep grief, there really aren't human words to express the way I feel and what I am experiencing. I can write to the best of my ability, but there just isn't a way to describe the reality of grief. The Bible tells me that the Holy Spirit prays for me at times like these. "We do not know what we ought to pray for, but the Spirit himself intercedes for us with groans that words cannot express. And he who searches our hearts knows the mind of the Spirit, because the Spirit intercedes for the saints in accordance with God's will" (Rom. 8:26–27).

These are spiritual words, not human words. They are on the tip of my tongue but not yet realized. They have meaning but can't be uttered, and they are deeper than my heart can reach. The words can't be found in my vocabulary or in a dictionary. They are sacred words that only God understands. Only when I get to heaven will I comprehend those words. My heavenly Father knows everything my heart can't communicate. He is the *deep* in my soul.

"Put out into deep water" (Luke 5:4). The disciples had fished all night and hadn't caught a thing. Jesus told them to throw out their nets into deeper water. When they did as He said, their nets were full and overflowing, nearly sinking their boats. And they were astonished. Why is it we think some things are impossible, even when God says nothing is impossible with Him? If only we would dig deeper into His word and go deeper in our prayers to know God more fully, then we would receive more supernatural sight and understand that, truly, nothing is impossible with God.

My struggles are teaching me valuable lessons in faith and trust. I think of Paul in 2 Corinthians, chapter 6, who related to us some of the deep valleys he endured, yet he persevered. In our afflictions, we can identify with Paul when he writes, "dying, and yet we live on; beaten, and yet not killed; sorrowful, yet always rejoicing; poor, yet making many rich; having nothing, and yet possessing everything" (v. 9–10). In the depths of my pain, will I not bear patiently God's will for my life and prove that my faith is real? Isn't this what the Christian life requires?

If you are experiencing a deep valley that is pulling you down to the lowest abyss, cry out to God. He is there. "Pour out your hearts to him, for God is our refuge" (Ps. 62:8b). The Enemy wants you to feel defeated. He wants to crush your faith and your hope. He wants you to despair of life. In Psalm 42:5–6, the writer asks, "Why are you downcast, O my soul? Why so disturbed within me? Put your hope in God, for I will yet praise him, my Savior and my God." We may feel depressed, but remembering that God is our hope and our Savior will help us go on.

Chapter 5

Digging Out

Answer me quickly, O LORD; my spirit fails. Do not hide your face from me or I will be like those who go down to the pit. Let the morning bring me word of your unfailing love, for I have put my trust in you. Show me the way I should go, for to you I lift up my soul (Ps. 143: 7–8).

God's promises are my daily bread. My heart, which cries out to God every morning, needs to be refreshed and reminded of His goodness. My weary soul needs the power of God to pick me back up and keep me going for another day.

Digging out is hard. It takes effort. It takes will. My experience has brought a clearer vision of my need for a sovereign God. When we are on the mountaintop and life is going well, we believe everything will be all right. But some of us aren't on those mountaintops. We are in the deepest valley our minds could ever imagine. Being in the dark valley is where we need comforters and fellow sufferers who understand that life is hard and isn't fair. We empathize with one another. We understand that just believing and having faith is sometimes easier verbalized than lived. We are part of the wounded who have sought and searched for God's heart and His promises on a daily basis so we don't surrender to despair. We dig in God's Word for strength and hope that only He can give as we continue our journey through loss. Our faith is an experienced faith and a tested faith. Our utterance of *everything will be all right,* will be realized only when we walk through heaven's gate.

Choosing to dig out is the brave way. If I may be so bold, choosing self-pity, despair, and bitterness is the coward's way. I know this because I have allowed myself to go there many times, too. How easy is it to be angry and bitter? I don't have to conjure up those emotions; they come naturally. They hang around like a dark cloud continuing to drag me further down into darkness. Wallowing in them produces self-pity, and self-pity comes from the pit of hell. Each time self-pity comes crashing into my life I must deny its power by digging out.

This isn't easy. The death of my child is a horror that fills my soul. My circumstances will either lead me to despair or guide me to God. There are only two choices, and I must choose one.

In the above Psalm, David wrote of his depression, feeling that he might die from his anguish. He is weary and worn and needs relief quickly. In another Psalm, he wrote, "Be merciful to me, O LORD, for I am in distress; my eyes grow weak with sorrow, my soul and my body with grief. My life is consumed by anguish and my years by groaning; my strength fails because of my affliction, and my bones grow weak" (Ps. 31:9–10).

When we find ourselves in the deep valleys of sorrow and loss, we need ongoing relief. Praying Scripture back to God may help us convey our deepest yearnings. Praying this Psalm to God helps me verbalize my own inner sorrow and relate to another sufferer. At times, we may be in such distress that we don't have the strength or effort of will to dig into the Scriptures. In such instances, be still and pour out your heart to God. Let Him minister to you as only He can. Let the Holy Spirit pray for you the words that you can't bring yourself to say or the feelings you can't put into words, (Rom. 8:26–27). Sometimes there are no known words to express the anguish of your heart.

During the cold days of January, four years and eight months after my son's passing, I found myself in a depressed state. I was downhearted and sad. I wished for circumstances that would never be. I compared my life to that of others my age and saw what I was missing. I had to do battle, digging my way through that. I read God's promises and believed them. I trusted Him, so why was the dark cloud hovering over and nearly consuming me? Despair is powerful, but hope is greater.

Paul said in 2 Timothy 4:7, "I have fought the good fight." He battled the circumstances of his life and had to dig continually to persevere, but he called it a "good fight." He could only call it good, knowing he fulfilled what God called him to do. In so doing, he "kept the faith." But it wasn't easy. His life required effort and ongoing, persistent work. He compared it to running a race. He completed the race successfully and, I believe, wrote this passage to encourage those of us who are struggling to hang in and keep digging.

Life is a battleground. God allows things to occur in our lives that we don't understand. The Enemy, the Devil, will do everything he can in these wars to convince us that God doesn't care. He will try to make us believe that, in all our troubles, we are going to fail, lose, and die. Yet, it is in these struggles that our faith becomes real and grows if we are digging into God's Word and praying for His strength and help.

In one of his messages, our pastor said that even in our dark days, "the potter never rests. He is constantly molding the clay."[1] God molds our character to fit the service He has for us. This encouraged me and made me realize that perhaps the sadness God had recently allowed had a purpose. Paul also wrote, "Can anything ever separate us from Christ's love? Does it mean he no longer loves us if we have trouble or calamity, or are persecuted, or hungry, or destitute, or in danger, or threatened with death? No, despite all these things, overwhelming victory is ours through Christ, who loved us" (Rom. 8:35, 37 NLT).

We can't achieve this victory on our own but only through the power of God. It wouldn't be called a victory if warfare weren't involved. The fight must be fought. Will our faith live or die in our battles? "So be strong and courageous, all you who put your hope in the Lord!" (Ps. 31:24 NLT).

God's love never leaves us. Keep holding on to Him, and He will lead us all the way home.

Chapter 6

Even Though

Even though I walk through the valley of
the shadow of death, I will fear no evil, for
you are with me; your rod and your staff,
they comfort me (Ps. 23:4).

Every struggle that Ed and I go through increases
awareness of our need for God. We had our future
planned differently. We talked often of taking our grandkids
camping and buying a larger vehicle to carry them around.
I read somewhere that you can write your plans in pencil,
but keep in mind that God has the eraser.

Our struggles seem to be unending. You never *get
over* losing a child. There seems to always be something
challenging us to persevere: Gary's friends marrying, having
babies, going on with their lives, and establishing themselves
in professions. The list doesn't stop there. It begins in
January and goes through December. With every season,

we experience various emotions. We have good memories, enjoyable days, sad days, and times of loneliness.

With every New Year, we are keenly aware that we are facing it without our son. However, we are that much closer to seeing him again. Every February, when my birthday rolls around, I wonder why I am still here and why God didn't take me instead. Yet, He is giving me another opportunity to direct a hurting world to Him.

Oh, the day the smallmouth bass starting biting! Nothing excited Gary more than spring fishing and tournaments. Patience is a virtue when it comes to this sport, and he had all he needed. He could fish all day and not catch anything. But his attitude was that it might come on the last cast. That usually paid off. I miss taking his pictures with all the fish he caught, but I enjoy the memories from the pictures I do have.

Since April was the month our son passed away, each day for a week, I relive what I experienced during that time. Easter was in April that year: the resurrection of our Lord, and because He lives, we also will live (John 14:19). Spring is bursting forth with new life, too. But, each April always brings me the strange realization that everything has changed.

Mother's Day is a bittersweet day. For me, it is a *mother without her child day*. While writing this, I witnessed a little three-year-old running to her grandmother and joyfully exclaiming, "Nana, Nana!" She squealed with excitement as her grandmother picked her up. The sight of that precious grandchild with her grandmother triggered a grief attack for me. Why, God, why? You took my only child and left me without the opportunity to ever become a grandmother. The pain is too much to bear today. I weep with sorrow and loss in my heart. Loss for something I will never experience; loss for my own son, who never had the opportunity to raise a family. Loss. Just loss. On the other hand, I have a precious mother who is still living, and I enjoy her and spending time with her.

At the beginning of every summer, we hold the Gary Lindsey Memorial Firecracker Fishing Tournament. Although it is a tremendous amount of work, the thought of keeping our son's memory alive is what motivates Ed. He puts forth everything he has because he feels like he is doing something for his son, and the need to do something for him never ends. We always donate the proceeds to a worthy organization in our son's memory and consider the tournament as a ministry. Father's Day is also this month. The tournament helps keep Ed's mind on something positive, instead of dwelling on his childlessness.

In summer, we also celebrate our wedding anniversary, the day our family began. Although our family is small, we are still a family. Now it is back to just the two of us, but it is a reminder of a good day.

When Gary was in school, sports always began when school did. Whether it was football or golf, we were heavily involved. We never missed a football game and rarely missed a practice. I walked many a golf course watching him play. I am so thankful that, whether it was sports, work, play, or worship, we were always there for him and actively involved in his life.

Deer season. The end of September is the beginning of bow season. Gary would look over all his equipment, see what he needed to buy or repair, make sure he had all the right camouflage and gear, and talk about it continually. I miss watching him prepare for this.

Gary's birthday is in October. A mother never forgets the day her baby is born. The day she sees him for the first time and experiences a love she never had before. We have such great memories of our son's life, and it all started in October.

For some reason, Thanksgiving is one of the hardest holidays for me. Maybe it is because we just celebrated his birthday, and it is right before Christmas. However, I have a memory of this month etched in my heart and mind that changes everything about death and loss. On November 14, 1995 at 8:00pm, Gary was saved and forever became a child of God. How remarkable that he wrote that date and time down in a book about hope. I am reminded of the verse from 1 Corinthians 15:54–55, "When the perishable has been clothed with the imperishable, and the mortal with immortality, then the saying that is written will come true: 'Death has been swallowed up in victory.' Where O death, is your victory? Where O death, is your sting?"

And finally, it's Christmas. A time when the family all comes together to celebrate Christ's birth, but someone is missing. Every member of our family feels Gary's absence.

Then it all starts over. At times, we feel we can't handle any more. We get tired. Struggling with grief is exhausting. I don't mean to sound gloomy or monotonous, but there is always something to contend with. On the other hand, there is always something good to remember. Each year that passes is a reminder that I am getting closer to seeing my son again. When what you love and value most has already gone on ahead of you to heaven, the attractiveness of this life lessens with each passing day.

The book of Habakkuk says, "Even though the fig trees have no blossoms, and there are no grapes on the vines; even though the olive crop fails, and the fields lie empty and barren; even though the flocks die in the fields, and the cattle barns are empty, yet I will rejoice in the LORD! I will be joyful in the God of my salvation!" (Hab. 3:17–18 NLT). Even though this life may not turn out how we planned, God has saved us through Jesus, and we have an eternal home waiting.

I heard Ed tell a friend how much our life has changed since Gary's death. This is mostly due to the fact that we have no other children or grandchildren on whom to focus. Our life was going along just fine, and then, abruptly, everything changed. We struggled to wrap our minds and hearts around the changes in our lives, but we couldn't go on the way things were. Our bodies and minds were in shock. What do we do now? Even after five years, we are still adjusting or readjusting to our changed way of life. This altered way was not in our plans. It wasn't what we chose, and it wasn't how we dreamed life would be at this point.

But here we are, and sometimes we don't know what to do or how to deal with things. God didn't ask if this is what we wanted. He didn't give us a choice, but this was His way for us. Sometimes we feel like we don't fit anywhere. We aren't empty nesters because this term is unpleasant to us. We aren't grandparents. We aren't a couple who never had children. We are childless parents.

Our young friends with children have been so sweet to always give us hugs and let us kiss their children. Our older friends are becoming grandparents and want to share them with us, too. I will never understand this side of heaven, why God deprived us of our one child and of becoming grandparents. My heart aches for what could have been but never will be. Our son remains constantly on our minds and in our hearts.

I'm sure there are those who feel we have moved on and are over our son's passing. It is a distant memory for them. So they may assume we feel the same. It reminds me of a verse from Proverbs 14:13 (NLT), "Laughter can conceal a heavy heart, but when the laughter ends, the grief remains." Our outward appearance doesn't always mirror our inward feelings. I don't expect people to think of our son the way we do, nor do I expect them to understand our grief and loss. I am reminded over and over that no one understands what we go through except those who have walked in our shoes.

I think of Job who lost all ten of his children. In the latter part of Job's life, the Lord blessed him more than ever (Job 42:12) giving him ten more children. Even though Job's life was great and was going well, don't you know he still grieved for those ten children? They couldn't be replaced, so God gave him more. Even though the Bible doesn't say so, I believe Job had times of mourning, until his last breath, for the children he lost.

It is so much easier to write about the trials of life and how to depend on God to get through them than it is to live them out. It is so easy to say *God is good* when you have not been through the fires of hell and wrestled with the question of *Is He really good?* It is so much easier to say, *Be thankful in everything* than it is to be thankful in a tragedy that has taken the life of your child. It is so much easier to say, *Rejoice in the Lord* when everything is good and going your way than it is to rejoice when your world has fallen apart, and you're trying to reconcile how God's perfect love fits into the horror of the darkest nights of your life.

We may not always like God's will, but it is *His* will. He hasn't asked if we only wanted the parts of His will that are good and to be spared the bad. When we have come to the place, like Job, who said, "Though he slay me, yet will I hope in him" (Job 13:15), or when we can say, "Your kingdom come, your will be done" (Matt. 6:10), regardless of what it is or how it affects your life, then we can truly obey the command, "be joyful in hope, patient in affliction, faithful in prayer" (Rom. 12:12).

For joy is not happiness but a confidence of knowing our salvation is secure. Happiness is based on circumstances. Joy is based on God's faithful promises. We are protected from anything that could snatch us out of the hand of God. We belong to Him, and nothing can change that. Tragedies can't change that. The deepest, darkest nights of your soul can't change that. Even when you feel He has abandoned you and is not holding you in the palm of His hand, you are still deeply loved and watched over.

Psalm 23:4 says that when we "walk through the valley of the shadow of death," God is with us. I have learned these truths by experience. I have wrestled with these statements until they have overtaken my heart. There is a verse of Scripture that I have come to identify with in a way that I never would have except through my experience. It is the phrase from 2 Corinthians 6:10, "sorrowful, yet always rejoicing." Another version says, "Our hearts ache, but we always have joy" (NLT). Even though it is hard for me to comprehend, I know I'm living this.

Here is my prayer.

Lord,

Since we have been appointed this sorrow in life, let it be useful. Grant us compassion so that we might minister to others, empathize with them, and point them to You. Give us strength to enjoy every occasion of growth and stage in Gary's friends' lives, celebrating and rejoicing with them. Bring to mind all the wonderful memories we have of our son as we take comfort in them. We thank You for his life and for allowing us the pleasure and joy of being his parents.

Chapter 7

Redeemed Suffering

Thou hast enlarged me when I was in distress (Ps. 4:1 KJV).

I desire to learn everything I can from my suffering. When I know a grief attack is coming on, or I have days of sadness, I do not try to run from it or escape the hold it has on me. By allowing myself to experience the suffering and embrace the pain, I can learn everything possible from it. During these times, I have seen God working in ways I never see on the better days. But my periods of mourning have not always been this way.

When we were planning Gary's funeral, I made the remark that God is God, and He has every right to take what He wants at any time. The pastor took those words and used them in the eulogy. Somewhere deep in my heart and soul, I knew this to be true and stated this with a great and strong faith. However, those words came back to test me when the reality of death and separation started setting in. In the anguish of my soul, I truly wanted to die. It was too difficult to live with this suffering. I was not so strong anymore. Where was my faith and where was God?

I remember when we were at the lake those three days and nights, begging God for my son's life, He didn't seem to respond. When I kept asking Him why, He didn't answer. All my days were dark, and He didn't relieve my pain. I was confused for being angry with God and doubting His goodness. This suffering that God allowed seemed unjust, not only for Ed and me, but for our son, too. I asked God, *What were You thinking? What were You trying to do?*

Out of utter helplessness, I searched the Bible for comfort, for anything that would calm my grief-stricken heart. And I found God was there. God knew my thoughts, my sadness, and my distress. He knew my doubts, my fears, and my frustrations. Everywhere I looked in the Bible, I would find words of reassurance and comfort, and I knew that God had never left me. I would have to learn to trust Him without understanding.

As I began to look back on that devastating experience with our son, I saw that God was there all along. During the three days at the lake, He was present through family and friends who wrapped us in prayer, provided food, and did anything they could for us. He was there through the rescue workers and the search crews who needed His help in finding our son. He was there. But not only was He there with us, He had been with our son every minute. God had never left his side.

The dark days are the ones when I sense Him the most now. They are the days my heart is full and overflowing with words of comfort for someone else. God wanted me to find Him for Himself and for no other reason. Not for what He could do for me, but just to "Be still, and know that I am God" (Ps. 46:10a). My perspective then changes, and instead of asking for deliverance from my suffering, I have accepted it as my new way of life. I can endure it because I know that, although God has withheld human understanding, He has enlarged my spiritual understanding. This suffering is redeemed, in that it now has purpose and can be used for God's glory. I know that my sorrows have worked for good and therefore raise me above my circumstances. There are eternal purposes at work. I could never use suffering for God's glory without having first plunged into the deepest depth of suffering.

Having lost our precious child, seeing our plans and his unravel and fade away and the desires of our hearts crushed, we must go another way now on this journey. We must trust God on a deeper level, knowing that we will persevere in suffering because there is a higher purpose. Although this grief has taken so much physical life out of me, it has made my soul stronger.

Jesus asked His disciples in the garden, "Could you not keep watch for one hour?" (Mark 14:37b). I hear Him asking me, *Can you not suffer a while longer? Here and now, it is time to carry your cross for My sake. Are you willing to take it up?* The cross I am called to bear is my very own. It is pointing a hopeless world to a Christ who is full of lasting hope. It is suffering loss. But it is redeemed. It is sacred. What is yours? What are you going to do with it?

Chapter 8

Entrusted with Sorrow

I would have despaired unless I had believed
that I would see the goodness of the LORD
(Ps. 27:13 NASB).

For so long, I tried to figure out God and why He would allow this tragedy in our lives. What was the purpose? What is the bigger picture? Did I cause this? Was it because of some past sins or disobedience? The questions never ended. I needed answers, but there were none. God has chosen not to explain Himself. And what can I say to that? He, alone, has that right. He answers to no one.

My conclusion to all my wonderings came to this: I can't figure it out. It's an aimless, disheartening circle of thoughts that goes nowhere. There's no point in trying to figure it out. But for some reason, I have to go through this cycle of trying to do so. I always end up right where I started, with no better understanding. I either believe God has a higher purpose, or I can believe He is out to get me, causing me to suffer for no apparent reason. I can believe that He is sovereign and more aware of my circumstances than I am, or that this is just part of an out-of-control world with no meaning and no supreme ruler. I can accept my calling in life, or I can reject an indiscernible purpose. Will my circumstance change if I choose not to follow God?

Profound sorrow can truly test your faith. There came a point where I had to choose which way I was going in life. In my choice I had an advantage; in my pain and loss I have experienced the presence of God in ways that I cannot ignore. Through my tears, He has revealed Himself in ways I have never experienced before. The same God who allowed my grief wants me to use it to draw others to Him. No, I don't understand, and this doesn't answer all my questions, but there is freedom in grasping this truth. Sorrow and loss have given my life a purpose.

Paul wrote in 2 Corinthians 1:3–4 that God is the "Father of compassion" who has granted us comfort so that we can comfort others. There are broken hearts everywhere. Suffering is worldwide and becoming more prevalent with each passing day. Our anguish calls out and a sovereign God hears our cries. He stands ready to comfort and strengthen us. Paul continued, "We were crushed and overwhelmed beyond our ability to endure, and we thought we would never live through it. In fact, we expected to die. But as a result, we stopped relying on ourselves and learned to rely only on God" (2 Cor. 1:8b–9a NLT). Oh, the great lesson of learning to rely only on God! Will He not give us everything we need to endure what He has allowed?

For some reason beyond my comprehension, God has entrusted me with sorrow. "Each one should retain the place in life that the Lord assigned to him and to which God has called him" (1 Cor. 7:17). Therefore, I choose to accept my lot in life and ask God to teach me through it. "In the course of my life he broke my strength" (Ps. 102:23a), to learn that He is my strength through my suffering and my hope for the future. I choose to believe; I choose to follow without knowing why.

In your loss, in your grief or pain, do not miss God. There are lessons to learn that you would never discover if not for your sufferings. Allow your experience to draw you closer to God. Take the opportunity for Him to minister to you and through you. He may not take your pain away. This is a time for drawing from God's measureless supply of grace and strength.

Chapter 9

My Heart Is in Heaven

The present seems so real; the unseen future seems so illusory. But in reality the opposite is true.

—Billy Graham [1]

So we fix our eyes not on what is seen, but on what is unseen. For what is seen is temporary, but what is unseen is eternal (2 Cor. 4:18).

We struggle with circumstances in this life that cause us pain and confusion. It is the here and now we are focused on because it is affecting us today. The more we look at our troubles, the more prone we are to fall into discouragement. It would be so easy to lose heart if this life were the final chapter. The Bible encourages us to not give up and to look beyond our present situation to the eternal, unseen, heavenly realms. We have a few glimpses of heaven from the Bible that were even difficult for the writers to describe.

Experiencing the darkest night of affliction caused me to reflect on heaven. Because Gary arrived there before us, we found ourselves fixated on our future home. What was it like? What was he experiencing? We started reading books on heaven. We searched the Scriptures on the subject of heaven. The thought of our son being somewhere we've never been stirred in us a great desire to be with him. The only way to see him again is for us to go to him.

When King David's baby son died, he said, "Can I bring him back again? I will go to him, but he will not return to me" (2 Sam. 12:23b). When God calls our name, we will be ready. We aren't afraid to die. Since our son has already experienced death, it somehow makes it easier for us. We have a desire to go home like never before.

I thought of heaven before my son went there. However, life is so busy that I didn't take the time to think deeply about the realities of heaven. I can't comprehend what heaven is truly like, but I know it exists. Having someone close to you die or become sick to the point of death can change your perspective on eternity and the things of God. You start thinking about what really matters in this life, which our pastor says "is the shortest part of eternity."[2]

And what really matters? We have a reason for being alive. There is a universal purpose in life—to love God and fulfill our part of His purposes. When we realize Jesus is everything, our outlook changes about what we do here on earth. He created us for Himself. Because Christ was resurrected, those who are in Him will also be resurrected.

Sometimes when Ed and I are together, I have a loneliness that enters my heart. It is for our son and our true home. I went a long time without mentioning this to him. One evening, while we were sitting in the swing in our quiet, peaceful backyard, this emotion came over me again. I wanted to tell him about it, so I said, "Sometimes I have this feeling, especially when we are together ..." But before I could finish the sentence he answered and said, "a lonely feeling." I said, "Yes! It's like for Gary and heaven." He said, "I have it, too." It's a loneliness we can't fill for each other. We yearn for our son and our real home, "for love is as strong as death" (Song 8:6).

Death is not the end; it is only the beginning of the longest part, the forever part. Each day we get a little closer to being there. I have found it crucial to my physical and mental health to fix my thoughts on Jesus and heaven. When I get there, I will see clearly everything that is so foggy here.

> Strive to be one of the few who walk this earth with the ever present realization – every morning, noon, and night – that the unknown that people call heaven is directly behind those things that are visible. [3]
>
> —L.B. Cowman

Until then, Ed and I ask God every day to give our son a hug and kiss and tell him how much we love and miss him. Sometimes I imagine Jesus walking up to Gary with a big smile on His face and Gary laughing and asking, "Another hug and kiss from Mom and Dad?" and Jesus reaching around him with a big hug and saying, "Of course!" Oh, the sweet thought of heaven.

Dear Son,

I was thinking about all the characteristics you had. From your Dad you learned to be friendly and outgoing. You never met a stranger, and those who knew you, loved you. You learned a good work ethic as you held jobs to support yourself and were responsible in those jobs. You were athletic and strong, able to run like a deer and react just as fast. In every sport you participated, you excelled. Like your dad, you were passionate about life and lived it with energy and enthusiasm. You seemed to notice and adopt all of your dad's best qualities.

From me you learned to smile and laugh. We did that a lot in our time together. You learned compassion and consideration for others. Even when you were a teenager, people would tell me what a gentlemen you were. You cried when life became heartrending for others. And on many occasions, you helped someone in need. Even though you were active and on the go, you learned to live leisurely, enjoying every minute. You acquired my physical features and tired of people always telling you, "You look just like your mother!" But that made me proud.

From both of us you learned to love the outdoors. You so enjoyed the lakes and the woods, the mountains and the streams. Cades Cove was one of your favorite places and you went there often. You learned to love God and His ways and knew the importance of being in church to meet with other believers.

I think often of your wonderful character and outgoing personality. I wonder what kind of work the Lord has you doing? I know that whatever it is, you are giving your all and glorifying Him. We love you, Son. Our hearts ache as we miss you with all our beings. One day, we will all be together again in heaven where our hearts are.

Chapter 10

Grace

We were crushed and overwhelmed beyond our ability to endure, and we thought we would never live through it. In fact, we expected to die. But as a result, we stopped relying on ourselves and learned to rely only on God, who raises the dead (2 Cor. 1:8b–9 NLT).

My grace is sufficient for you, for my power is made perfect in weakness (2 Cor. 12:9).

Grace. God's grace is beyond my understanding. I have thought about His grace, read about His grace, and experienced an abundance of it. Nevertheless, I can't explain the depths of grace. His grace was with me when my life was going well, and it was there when my world fell apart. Grace is a gift from God. His grace brought salvation, even though we don't deserve it. He graces all of us with good things every day, not just His children; His graces reach everyone. Furthermore, His grace brings believers peace that assures us He will help us in our afflictions. Grace is a wonderful gift.

Each day, people muster up enough self-sufficient courage and confidence to get through their hurts. They take a positive outlook and try their best to help themselves. They focus on their natural abilities to produce strength and calmness in their lives. They may live their whole lives this way and make it through without ever seeking God. But they have missed out on recognizing one of God's greatest gifts.

After Gary's passing and the daily awareness of living with loss, I did not think I would survive. I felt too weak and helpless. What was life going to be like now? How could I possibly endure this suffering? The emptiness in my soul needed filling. There was a point at which I would not have been able to gather the will to carry on in my natural state. I needed the supernatural hand of God. If this was the path God chose for my life, surely He could grant me the grace to endure it.

God works best through our weaknesses. This knowledge came home to me the first time someone said, "You are such a strong woman!" My immediate thought was *What is she talking about? I am so weak!* I was shocked by the comment and oblivious that I had proved to be strong. This happened many times over, and not just to me, but also to Ed and me as a couple. Our pastor has reiterated the statement, "The Christian life is not us living for Jesus, but Jesus living in and through us."[1] Jesus' strength was flowing through us and we didn't even notice. Our weaknesses gave God a means through which to display His power in our lives. It is Jesus living in and through us. If I tried to make myself strong and show confidence in my flesh, there would be no glory for God.

We have chosen to be His broken vessels and to rely on Him. Then He raises us from the dead state of lifeless grief and helps us to live with our suffering in ways that show His power. He restores our soul to worship and praise Him, even on the hardest days. This is the part I can't comprehend because it is supernatural. It is from heaven. God has taught me that His grace *is* sufficient. My life is living proof of it.

Chapter 11

In the Garden

I am the true vine, and my Father is the gardener. He cuts off every branch in me that bears no fruit, while every branch that does bear fruit he prunes so that it will be even more fruitful (John 15:1–2).

My flower gardens are my therapy. Digging in the ground and planting flowers slows down my mind. When Ed tills up the vegetable garden spot, I absorb the smell of fresh dirt. There's something wholesome about that smell. In Gary's memory garden, there is a wicker loveseat that I use to sit and think or admire the beautiful roses and other plants given to us by friends and family. It is a peaceful place. If it were never cared for and taken over by weeds, it wouldn't be that way. It would be annoying if I had to fight my way through grass and weeds. But I have cared for my garden; therefore, it thrives.

Not all my gardens are like this one. After Gary's accident, Ed and I had little motivation to do anything. Our minds were consumed with grief that left us depressed. Besides the memory garden, I left the others unattended. Then winter came with long, dark nights and cold dreary days. We stayed in much of the time. We didn't want to go anywhere or be in crowds. It was just too hard. During the cold days of February, I noticed buttercups coming up amongst the weeds in one of my backyard, unattended gardens. I stood and looked at them but had no incentive to do anything. It was an ugly sight.

My flowerbed in the front yard was a mess, too. Summer had produced so many flowers that everything ran together. The paths were overgrown and everything was disorganized. It was too crowded. But I couldn't find the drive to fix it.

Our yard has large trees that provide shade in the summer. I love my trees. But in the fall of the year that Gary passed away, Ed declared they were going to have to be trimmed. I put up a fuss. In my grief, they were a comfort to me and to trim them was upsetting. Even when he trimmed the bushes, it distressed me. Now he wanted to hack my trees! I cried the whole time they were being cut back.

I had become so despondent that I knew something had to be done. I was dying on the inside. I felt God nudging me to go outside. *Lord, I feel like You have plowed my soul. You've broken me up and I'm hurt.* The thought then came more urgently, *Go outside.* I grabbed a shovel and dug up the front flowerbed. This took several hours, but I felt better after having accomplished that task. Then I reworked it and placed new plants in a better design. This kept my mind busy, though my thoughts never left my son. This task gave me more positive thoughts.

In summer, one of my favorite things to do is deadhead my garden. Cutting off the old blooms helps produce new ones and makes a more attractive plant. Sometimes the branches on the roses turn yellow and have to be pruned back, or it takes over the whole bush. There is something therapeutic in deadheading and pruning. I am alone in the quietness with my thoughts. It's like the old song about walking and talking with God in the garden. I feel close to God there.

Jesus says He prunes me so that I can be more like Him, and pruning produces godly character in me. Sometimes it hurts, and I don't understand why He had to cut so hard. Why did He have to take away my comfort for a time? Why did He let me think He had deserted me by cutting me to the quick? He says, even though He prunes, chops, and cuts, to leave us to wilt and die is not what He desires. He wants us to trust Him and remain with Him, for without Him, we cannot produce anything (John 15:5). In response to this realization, I wrote a poem.

My bloom is of sorrow,
Of loss, and pain.
Why have you cut me?
For Your great gain?

Oh, how the knife
Does hurt to the core.
How far will You break—
Very much more?

Janet Lindsey

You are the vine;
Help me cling to.
Don't let me fall,
But take hold of You.

So even in grief,
My lot it is;
My gardener is mine
And I am His!

Chapter 12

All about Fish

"Friends, haven't you any fish?" "No," they answered. "Throw your net on the right side of the boat and you will find some." When they did, they were unable to haul the net in because of the large number of fish (John 21:5–6).

Gary loved to watch fishing on television. He didn't just watch it for entertainment, either. It was educational for him. He learned about new or different ways to catch more and larger fish. One of his favorite professional fishermen has a contagious laugh. Whenever he catches a good fish, he usually kisses it before throwing it back. Although he was entertaining, Gary knew to pay attention to the details.

Gary read a devotional centered on fishing that he'd had since he was twelve. In a section of the book for notes, Gary had written that you shouldn't switch lures too often;

you probably won't catch as many fish. And believe that fish fall from heaven because they can, and they do. I didn't look through the book and find these words until a couple of years after his passing. I always wondered where Gary got the idea of fish falling from heaven.

Today, as I was sitting in my office, I looked up and saw the book on the bookshelf. I was reminded of what he wrote but was prompted to take the book down and look through it again. There was one page earmarked that I don't remember noticing before. In this devotional, the writer talked about his wife winning numerous fishing tournaments and about how fish would often seemingly fall from heaven at just the right time. There was also a prayer at the end of the devotion thanking God for victories in fishing tournaments and for the eternal hope we have in Jesus. No wonder he earmarked this page. I can understand why the book spoke to him, or any fishing person.

Gary had another interpretation that he also wrote in the book. He wrote, "Choose God's lure, and you'll be headed in the right direction." Before we knew Gary had written that, we decided to play a song at his funeral entitled, *Keep Your Lure in the Water.* It's a song about keeping God first and luring others to Him. Our fishing tournament event T-shirt every year has the slogan, "Keep your lure in the living waters of Jesus Christ."

After Jesus spoke to a crowd from Simon's boat, he told him to, "Put out into deep water, and let down the nets for a catch." Simon answered, "Master, we've worked hard all night and haven't caught anything. But because you say so, I will let down the nets" (Luke 5:4–5). This is when Jesus first called his disciples. They knew who He was and had listened to His teaching. Now Jesus was calling them to go deeper with Him and to know Him intimately.

"Put out into deep water." Follow Him wherever He leads. Through good times, hard times, and tragic times. Even unto death. Know Him and draw from Him. Dig deep for Him.

"We've worked hard all night." We try using our excuses, our second thoughts, our own way, and our own strength— all to no avail.

"But because you say so." I surrender to Your will. I obey. I give up the right to my plans and myself. I will follow You, Lord. Although I may not see the outcome or the purpose for my labor, I will persevere. I will hope in You.

"They caught such a large number of fish that their nets began to break. So they signaled their partners in the other boat to come and help them, and they came and filled both boats so full that they began to sink" (Luke 5:6–7). There was no denying that this was a miracle and they "were astonished" (v. 9). The fishermen understood this miracle more than those on the shore did. Jesus was relating to them as fishermen in the best way they could understand. They had never caught fish like this. Jesus comes to us in ways we understand and brings us to acknowledge our helpless and sinful state apart from Him. We have great need of a Savior.

"Then Jesus said to Simon, 'Don't be afraid; from now on you will catch men'" (v. 10). God's plan for the disciples was to catch men. This was their new way of life; they obeyed and followed. I believe if they could have seen the end at the beginning, they still would have followed. The end was that most of them died cruel, horrific deaths because of their faith in Jesus. They lived and died for the sake of Christ.

"So they pulled their boats up on shore, left everything and followed him" (v. 11). Jesus asks us to do no less. It's time to cast the lure out into the deep water and see the catch He brings in.

Chapter 13

The God Things II

In my first book, *Peering through a Mist*, I wrote a chapter entitled *The God Things* about the many astounding ways God had shown Himself to others and to us through our experience of loss. I believe when we keep our eyes open to God working, we will see Him move. This is not just my belief but a biblical principle. "But blessed are your eyes because they see, and your ears because they hear" (Matt. 13:16).

The Lord has allowed me to see Him work when my spiritual eyes were open. I can't help but wonder what I missed when I was overtaken by the cares of the world and the busyness of life. Regrettably, many times we allow worldly things to get between the Lord and us. At times we need quietness in our life in order to hear God speaking. The television, our phones, and just everyday noises replace blessings when we allow them to permeate our lives. That is why it is so important to have a quiet time with God, a set-apart time to refocus and replenish our spiritual, emotional, mental, and physical well-being with the one who can restore in us what we need.

When our spiritual eyes and ears are open and we see God working, our faith is increased. Regardless of what is going on in our lives, He is always working to bring us closer to Him. God has worked supernatural connections in my life, and I want to share some of them in order that He might be praised.

My sister, Laura, has a boutique. For the first year, it was in a small strip mall along a busy intersection. Some days were busy, while others were extremely slow and boring. I would help her on days when she couldn't be there. After publishing my first book, we held a book signing at the boutique. That day I met others who had experienced loss, and we shared tears and hugs. This was expected, since the signing was advertised. Nevertheless, I heard stories of others' tragedies and formed a bond with other grievers.

One day when I was there by myself, a lady came in and asked if the owner was in. She wanted to display a product she was selling. I explained that Laura would be in shortly, and she decided to wait. She was browsing through the shop and talking about the merchandise, when out of nowhere, she said, "My son died."

I thought, *did she just say what I thought she said*? So I asked, "What?"

She answered, "My son died." This led to a conversation about her son's battle against cancer and having to watch him slowly die. Until we shared our stories, she had no idea that I had lost a son. This was just an amazing way of God bringing us together. She had a book she thought I would like to read. So we exchanged books. When Laura came in, I told her about the lady and she was amazed. Laura allowed her to display her products, and the lady returned on a regular basis. As a result, they became friends.

And there was another griever. She came into the boutique to purchase a gift for her best friend who was flying in the next morning. She wanted to give her a good taste of East Tennessee Volunteer country by buying something orange. She chose her gifts, and while Laura and I were wrapping them, she told us she lived in Nebraska but had grown up in Knoxville. Her mother was sick, and she was here to help her for a while. Again, in the middle of this conversation out of nowhere, she said, "I lost my son."

Laura and I exchanged glances and I asked, "You lost your son?" She began telling us what a horrible day she was having. Her son died in February, only a little over two months before. He had a disease and died suddenly. He lived away from her, and when he did not answer or return her calls, she knew something was wrong. Now she was struggling with not being there for him when he needed her most.

I understood this completely. She is a believer, as was her son. She knew he was with Jesus, but the separation was agonizing. I said, "I lost my son, too." She threw her hand over her chest and asked me some questions about it. We all three started crying. Her tears were like a waterfall. We hugged many times. Her pain was fresh. She wanted to die and even said this to her remaining son. But he told her he needed her, and this is what kept her going. She apologized repeatedly for her tears and told herself to breathe. When I think back on this lady, it's her river of tears I remember most. And God "will wipe every tear from their eyes" (Rev. 21:4).

A week or so later, she came in the shop again, this time with her friend. Her friend had encouraged her just by being with her, and she was in a better way this day.

Several of our local churches had joined together to hold revivals during the same week. The minister who came to our church was funny and a true man of God. After hearing his sermon one evening, I came home and sat in the swing on my patio. I was reflecting on what he said, while thinking about my son. I turned to my right, looked up in the sky, and saw a cross, probably made from two airplanes crossing paths; the backdrop was a pink sky. I knew it was there for me as a comforting reminder that my son was alright, and the cross is the reason why.

Also during these revivals, a friend who attends a different church had listened to a minister tell about losing his teenage son in a car wreck. When the service was over, the friend told the minister about Ed and me and the book I had written about the loss of our son. The minister called that week and asked to meet with us. We sat in a coffee shop for several hours one night talking about our boys and how the Lord had given us strength and comfort. We found a new friend in grief that night.

One day I received a letter from one of Gary's high school friends. She wrote to tell me how much she loved Gary like a brother. She recalled some of the dramatic stories he would tell in art class about his hunting adventures, going into detail about things a girl really doesn't want to hear. She talked about his smile and how everyone loved him. She said she was jealous because he went to heaven and the rest of his friends were *stuck* here. I laughed and cried while reading this letter. It saddened me yet was comforting at the same time. I'm so thankful a young person took the time to tell Gary's mom how much he meant to his friends.

During the sign-ups for the fifth annual fishing tournament, a young man mentioned that several years ago, Gary showed him the right bait to fish with and even took him fishing. We didn't know anything about this fishing trip, but the guy was grateful that Gary invested his time to help someone else experience the joys of fishing. Many people have shared a story about how Gary showed kindness toward them. These memories have helped Ed and me so much with our grief, knowing our son was considerate and thoughtful of others.

During that tournament, rain was predicted for the entire day. The tournament began at 7: 00 p.m. and ended at 7:00 a.m. But preparation and registration required us to be there the whole day before the tournament started. This was the first year we would experience bad weather. The year before, it had been a beautiful day, although it got up to 105 degrees. While at the lake all day, we watched rain from a distance circle all around us. Showers would pop up toward the east or west but never make it to us. People would comment that it poured on the way, and it was coming in our direction, but it never did. Besides a brief, light shower at midafternoon, there was no rain and no storm.

We were so thankful that God protected our spot at the lake. All that night there were chances of rain, too, but we didn't have any. The next morning after the tournament concluded, and the tents were taken down, and everything was cleaned up, we got into our cars and began pulling out together. Suddenly, the sky opened up, and it literally poured the rest of the day. We knew the Lord had done that just for us!

At the sixth annual tournament, we had a downpour of rain right before the boats were to blast off. As soon as it stopped raining, God gave us a beautiful rainbow.

After I wrote the first book, I commented that I had said everything I wanted to say and would not be writing another. However, the Lord kept on impressing upon my heart words I felt might benefit someone else. As the Lord has helped me, surely I could help others in their grief.

I started taking notes until I had so many that I felt overwhelmed. I continued to pray and ask for guidance, even when I was sure this was what He wanted me to do. However, I was attacked with negative thoughts every time I would pray. *You're not qualified. You are so inadequate. Who wants to read what you have to say?* I really didn't have the ability, but I learned with the first book that "nothing is impossible with God" (Luke 1:37). And I held to the promise from Hebrews 13:21 reminding us that Jesus equips us with everything we need to do His will. I was willing and available to do what He wanted.

One morning, out of my humanness, I pleaded one more time with the Lord to confirm that this was what He wanted me to do. Within a week, I received an e-mail from a man in Alabama who led a grief support group from his church. He told me they were purchasing my book, distributing it within the group, and discussing several chapters. He told me of his experience with losing his wife, and leading this group was a way to help others with his grief. He wanted to know where he could purchase more books. That was my confirmation. God was connecting me with other sufferers who were reaching out to give hope to the hopeless and comfort to the grieving through Jesus Christ.

Later I found two Facebook messages sent months before from women who had lost children and who had read my book. The messages somehow got lost in my message box because we were not friends on Facebook. I felt bad and responded to them immediately, explaining why I had not seen them. They told me of their loss and how reading my book had helped them in their grief. We have since become friends through Facebook and message each other occasionally.

Ed was working at a fishing show in a nearby city when a man approached him and asked if he could talk a few minutes. In their conversation the man told Ed that he had known our son from fishing tournaments. He said that during the search and rescue for Gary, he had piloted one of the helicopters in the air search. He was sorry for our loss.

On another occasion, Ed and I had to purchase a new lawn mower from an equipment store. A man standing near me was making a purchase. He heard my name mentioned and asked if I was Gary's mother. When I told him yes, he explained that he was a diver for search and rescue and had searched and dived for our son over the three days and nights he was missing. He said he was there when they found him. I gave him a big hug and thanked him for risking his life to find our son.

What was unusual about meeting this diver (because there were several divers) was that two years prior, when I published my first book, my sister asked me to sign a book for him. She was going to deliver it to his wife, whom she had known from her daughter's school. When I signed the book, I also enclosed a card thanking him for everything he had done to help find our son. This day, when we finally met and talked, he told me that he had just read the card again. We always remember those who were involved in the search and rescue and take every opportunity we can to thank them again.

While shopping at a local store, I befriended the clerk who always checks me out. She is a Christian, and our conversations are usually about the Lord. I awoke one night thinking about her. I felt I should take her one of my books. The next day, I went into the store to find her and she wasn't there. As I was walking back to my car, she was getting out of hers to come to work. I told her I was there just to see her and give her a book. I explained that I had written it after losing my son. I knew she was a Christian and thought she might like to read it. Thanking me, we parted ways.

Sometime later when I was at the store again, she told me that while she was reading the book, she realized this was the young man and family for whom the Lord had urged her to pray. She passed the search and rescue site each time she went to work and had prayed for us, not even knowing who we were. She was thankful to finally know for whom she prayed and how God had allowed us to meet.

Chapter 14

Last Part

> We should live in this evil world with
> wisdom, righteousness, and devotion to
> God, while we look forward with hope to
> that wonderful day when the glory of our
> great God and Savior, Jesus Christ, will be
> revealed (Titus 2:12b–13 NLT).

Time is running out. There is urgency in our days like never before. I sense it, too. Not only are our days coming to an end because we grow older every day and will one day pass on, but the time for Jesus' return is closer. So whichever comes first, life as we know it is coming to an end. The Bible tells us about Jesus' return in Mark 13:32–33, "No one knows about that day or hour, not even the angels in heaven, nor the Son, but only the Father. Be on guard! Be alert! You do not know when that time will come."

I see people going through this life who never acknowledge God. They think they are doing just fine, and certainly, they may manage without knowing a living Savior. However, I would challenge them to carefully examine their hearts. There is a longing in every human heart for someone larger than us, a sovereign deity. The Bible says we have no excuse for not knowing or honoring God because of His creation (Rom. 1:20, Ps. 19:1–2).

It is arrogant to think death could not happen to us today. What if Jesus retrieves His redeemed ones today? We have no such wisdom or insight into the future and God's orchestrating of time and events. We are clueless about how much time we have on earth. We may not even have the rest of the day. My son is an example of that. We talked of his plans only a few minutes before his life was over. We have an ordained day to be born and a day to die; no timetable came with our birth certificates alerting us of that fact.

See with the eyes of your heart. Our times are not in our hands; they are in God's (Ps. 31:15). Who of us can add a week, a day, or even an hour to our life? Do we control our destiny? These are questions that need to be answered today. It is selfish pride that keeps putting off Jesus. There are only two ways and one choice—God's way or not. I pray you will choose God through His Son, Jesus, who loves you so much, that He died for you. He took our sins on the cross upon Himself so that we could be forgiven, set free, and have straight access to God the Father. He offers life eternal in heaven. Some are waiting for tomorrow or a changed lifestyle or perhaps a time when they aren't so busy. "I tell you, now is the time of God's favor, now is the day of salvation" (2 Cor. 6:2b).

Jesus said, "I am the way and the truth and the life. No one comes to the Father except through me" (John 14:6). He is the only way to salvation. You may say it is narrow-minded to believe there is only one way. Jesus said it. I just believe what He said. "I am the gate; whoever enters through me will be saved" (John 10:9). Jesus is passionate about us and wants to live in a relationship with us.

Paul said, "If Christ has not been raised, your faith is futile; you are still in your sins ... But Christ has indeed been raised from the dead" (1 Cor. 15:17, 20). Therefore, we have hope in a living Christ. There is no lasting hope apart from Christ. He is our only hope. When you set your hope on Him, you will not be disappointed.

This life can be so hard. Throughout history, there is heartache and grief, pain and suffering, sickness and death. There is no escaping affliction in this life. Bad news is everywhere. But you can survive with hope. "Remember your word to your servant, for you have given me hope. My comfort in my suffering is this: Your promise preserves my life" (Ps. 119:49–50).

God hasn't freed me from my grief. But in it, and because of it, He is continually showing me in His word that He is aware of my sorrow. He does this by answering my prayers and through uplifting experiences with other people. He knows my every thought and all the reasons my heart hurts. He has comforted me and given a peace that is beyond my understanding. Even in the dark days, I can say I am at rest in Jesus. He is my Rock and my hope.

"For this God is our God for ever and ever; he will be our guide even to the end" (Ps. 48:14). When I arrive in heaven, I'm sure I will see how God orchestrated my life for His purposes through loneliness, trials, heartache, disappointments, and grief, as well as through joy, blessings, love, and the good days. "The LORD will fulfill his purpose for me; your love, O LORD, endures forever" (Ps. 138:8).

Some may ask, *What good can come from great loss?* Oftentimes, when a young person dies, the effect it has on their friends and family influences them more than when a person in their eighties passes away. We expect to die when we are old. The loss of the young is more tragic because of all the possibilities before them and the severing of years of life ahead of them. I have, however, witnessed changed lives in many. Ed and I have been able to comfort others and give back appreciation in ways that were never possible before our loss. We have drawn our strength and comfort from the Lord and have drawn closer in our relationship to Him. We have found grace sufficient until our dying day.

The greatest tragedy would be to live a useless, self-indulgent, purposeless life, full of pride, with the thought that God owes us something. To miss Jesus in this life is to miss life eternal with Him. Our life is a vapor, and it fades away a little more each day. Only what we have done for Jesus will stand because life is all about Him.

Sometimes the pain and heartache in life can seem overwhelming. Our storms are meant to draw us closer to the God of hope and His provisions. We read of people in the Bible many times over who thought their circumstances were hopeless. Yet when they came to the end of themselves in their darkest hour and cried out to the Lord, they found He was there.

In Acts 27:13–44, we find Paul enduring a dreadful storm as a prisoner on a ship. Along with him were the crew, Luke, and other prisoners. When the storm became overpowering, they began to throw the cargo and tackle overboard to lighten the ship. "When neither sun nor stars appeared for many days and the storm continued raging, we finally gave up all hope of being saved" (v. 20).

I couldn't help but remember my grief when I felt like a heavy load was bearing down on my heart. When there was no light in my soul or seemingly any future hope ahead for Ed and me. When I felt like just giving up and lying down to die. Until those words, "Because of the LORD'S great love, we are not consumed" (Lam. 3:22) fell on my heart one morning. Then I began to see a glimmer of hope and began pouring out my heavy heart to God.

In the next few verses of Acts 27, we see God giving Paul strength to encourage the others, "So keep up your courage … for I have faith in God" (v. 25). Paul and his companions all made it to safety. And those of us who have placed our trust in the living God will also make it to safety, to our final destination, which is heaven. He is able to give you the strength to carry on. He promises in Scripture that He is the God of peace and comfort. This is the hope we possess as our very own. God will not leave us or forsake us. Take courage in this. Find strength in this to go on and fulfill His purpose in your life for His glory.

> Yet this I call to mind and therefore I have hope: Because of the LORD'S great love we are not consumed, for his compassions never fail. They are new every morning; great is your faithfulness" (Lam. 3:21-23).

Notes

Chapter 5
Digging Out
1. Jim Cummings, Dotson Memorial Baptist Church, Maryville, Tennessee. Used by permission.

Chapter 9
My Heart Is in Heaven
1. Reprinted by permission. *Hope for Each Day*, Billy Graham, Copyright © 2002, Thomas Nelson Inc. Nashville, Tennessee. All rights reserved.
2. Jim Cummings, Dotson Memorial Baptist Church, Maryville, Tennessee. Used by permission.
3. Taken from *Streams in the Desert* by L.B. Cowman, Copyright © 1997 by Zondervan. Used by permission of Zondervan. *www.zondervan.com*.

Chapter 10
Grace
1. Jim Cummings, Dotson Memorial Baptist Church, Maryville, Tennessee. Used by permission.